I'd like to dedicate this book to the following
primary schools, where I have been Patron of Reading.
I've loved working with you all.

shill Hall, Rosslyn Park,
Ambleside (Nottingham), Devonshire Road (Bolton),
Northcote (Liverpool), Whinney Banks (Middlesbrough)

JANETTA OTTER-BARRY BOOKS

Crazy Classrooms collection copyright © Paul Cookson 2015
*Champion of the School, Crazy in Our Class, The Day that Miss Went Missing
and Sir Just Wasn't There, Dear Headteacher, Don't Go in the Changing Rooms,
The First Snow on the Playground, Fly Away Teacher, How to Hide at School,
I Just Don't Trust the Furniture, It's Hard Being a Jehovah's Witness at Christmas,
Just Jacko, The Kitchen Regrets the Inconvenience Caused, Lunchpack Flapjack
Snack Attack, Mr Radar's Ears, Mothers' Day Cards, The Office Manager,
On Our School Class Photograph, Our Teacher is a Tongue Twister, The
Reasons Why, Shoes, Thumb-Thing's Up, The Ties That Blind, Twelve Inventions
to Help You Survive at School, Twenty Teachers at our School, Visitors Beware,
When the Teacher Turns Their Back* copyright © Paul Cookson 2015
All other poems copyright © Paul Cookson 2001, first published in
Crazy Classrooms, Secret Staffrooms, Lion Publishing PLC, 2001
Illustrations copyright © Steve Wells 2015

This edition first published in Great Britain and in the USA in 2015 by
Frances Lincoln Children's Books, 74-77 White Lion Street,
London N1 9PF
www.franceslincoln.com

A catalogue record for this book is available from the British Library.

ISBN 978-1-84780-505-8

Printed and bound by CPI Group (UK) Ltd, Croydon, CR0 4YY

1 3 5 7 9 8 6 4 2

Poems by
PAUL COOKSON

Drawings by
STEVE WELLS

Frances Lincoln
Children's Books

CONTENTS

Crazy in our Class

Paul and Peter pulling faces
Ruth and Rachel running races
Thompson twins changing places
Crazy in our class

Laura's laugh is really weird
William's wind is really feared
Shaun's shorts have disappeared
Crazy in our class

Fifty footballs on the floor
Bags for goalposts by the door
Nobody is keeping score
Crazy in our class

All the girls style their hair
Boys show off their underwear
Whoopee cushions on the chair
Crazy in our class

You can hear us in the hall
We're the worst class of them all
Drive our teacher up the wall
Crazy in our class

Crazy, crazy, crazy
Crazy in our class

The First Day After the Holidays

Is always the best.
You get to see all your friends again
and catch up on the news.

Nobody does much work,
just writing your name on a new exercise book
and nobody sets homework.

You don't get told off
for not having your PE kit
and the breaks are often longer.

Yes, the first day after the holidays
is always the best,
apart from the day we break up.

On the second day
it always feels like you've never been away
and holidays seem an eternity ago.

What The Head Always Says When Introducing The Visiting Poet

Well children
We are very lucky today
Because we have got a SPECIAL VISITOR today

Can you see a strange face in assembly this morning?
Can you see our SPECIAL VISITOR?

Hands up if you know his name
Hands up if you know what our SPECIAL VISITOR
    does for a job?

No ... he's not the Vicar
No ... he's not a fireman

He's an AUTHOR
Do you know what an author does?

Yes, David ... I know your grandad is called Arthur
But Mr Cookson is an AUTHOR
And he writes books
But not ordinary books
He writes SPECIAL books
Books of POETRY
Do you know what POETRY is?
No, David - it's not chickens
That's poultry

Because it's our book week
We are very lucky today
We have a got a REAL LIVE POET.

First Day New Class Blues

All alone and by myself
At the back, on the shelf
Wishing I was somewhere else
The first day new class blues.

I don't know where I should be
No one wants to sit by me
On my own till half past three
The first day new class blues.

No one says a single word
Nothing that I say is heard
I'd speak louder but I'm scared
The first day new class blues.

There's nobody here I know
Time just seems to pass so slow
I can't wait for the bell to go
The first day new class blues.

I just want to make one friend
I think I'm going round the bend
I can't wait for the day to end
The first day new class blues.

Perhaps tomorrow won't be bad
Perhaps then I won't be so sad
Perhaps it's just that I have had
The first day new class blues.

On our School Class Photograph

Frantic at the front and chaos at the back
Madness rules in the middle of the pack
Anarchy, mayhem, everybody daft
On our school class photograph.

Billy's blowing bubbles, Paula's pulling hair
Tina's tongue twirls everywhere
Colin cranes his neck just like a giraffe
On our school class photograph.

Luka's back to front, Deepa's upside down
Leroy looks up while Ella starts to frown
Neville needs a hairbrush, Jimmy needs a bath
On our school class photograph.

Marie-Anne's a model — too much make-up
Dopey Derek's sleeping, he can't seem to wake up
Lee - he sneers like a psychopath
On our school class photograph.

Half the class are riff while the other half are raff
Everybody smirking, trying not to laugh
If you think the kids look bad – you should see the staff
On our school class photograph.

The Teachers' Secret Boring Sock Shop

There are long socks, short socks,
Woolly socks, cotton socks
In the fully stocked shop
That stocks the teachers' socks.

Boxes storing boring socks
Stacks of packs of brown and blacks
Grey socks stacked on top of racks
Guaranteed not to shock.

Diamond-patterned short socks
Plain white sports socks
Nothing with a daft design
Or trendy fashion feature.

Don't defy convention socks
Do not draw attention socks
Nothing garish or nightmarish
Nothing flashy, nothing brassy.

Nothing tasteless, ostentatious,
Nothing glaring, nothing daring,
Very normal, very formal,
Very thermal, very warmal,

Non alluring very boring socks for boring teachers.

The Ties That Blind

Monday's tie is pink and spotty
Tuesday's tie is green and grotty

Wednesday's tie is rainbow flowers
Thursday's – hypnotising powers

Friday's kipper tie's the worst
Looks like all the paints have burst

We all need to wear dark glasses
When our teachers takes our classes

A wardrobe that will hypnotise
Don't stare at our teacher's ties

They're the worst that he can find
Our teacher wears the ties that blind

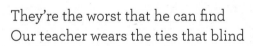

TWENTY TEACHERS AT OUR SCHOOL

The music teacher with no rhythm ... Mister Beet

The English teacher who gets things wrong ... Miss Take

The supply teacher who teaches all the subjects ...
Miss Ellaneous

The exotic dance teacher ... Ms Merising

The PE teacher who cannot score a goal ...
Mister Nother-Sitter

The Geography teacher ... Miss Issippi

The depressing French teacher ... Miss Eree

The teacher nobody knows ... Mister E.

The teacher no one understands ... Mister Fy

The Italian teacher troubled by insect bites ... Miss Quito

The drama teacher ... Ms Kerade

Two Religious Studies teachers ... Miss Belief
and Ms Iah

The Head of Science who always speaks his mind ...
Professor Pinnion

The very attractive student teacher who everyone wants
to kiss ... Miss Eltoe

The outdoor pursuits teachers who were once stuck on
a desert island ...Miss Adventure and Miss Ageinabottle

The CDT teacher no one really knows anything
about apart from the fact that she's good with wood ...
Miss Teak

The music teacher who writes choruses for
competitions never knowing what he may win ...
Mister Reprise

The Greek teacher who looks like Medusa but instead
of snakes she has feathers ...Miss Tickle-Beast

Mrs Kenning

Loud shouter
Deep thinker
Rain hater
Coffee drinker

Spell checker
Sum ticker
Line giver
Nit picker

Ready listener
Trouble carer
Hometime lover
Knowledge sharer

The Office Manager

She is not the Secretary
She's the Office Manager
Only trouble is ...
Nobody can manage her

Her bark is bad, her bite is worse
Questions later, shouting first
Just one thing to remember
Don't ask for Blu-tack in September

Need more than a pinch of salt
Everything is not her fault
Everybody knows their place
Do not take her parking space!

Nothing louder, nothing clearer
You can always, always hear her
Even dinner ladies fear her
All the teachers daren't go near her

Indestructa-bullet-proof
Nothing much can damage her
She thinks she truly rules the school
She's the Office Manager

Our Teacher Is A Tongue Twister

Our teacher's strangest feature
Is his tongue that's strong and long
Like a big red carpet it unrolls
And what we like the most
Is when he's feeling gross
He sticks it out and shoves it up his nose

We can see it slide and squirm
Like a wibbly dribbly worm
Oozing slime and drooling where it goes
But his bestest ever trick
Is the one that makes us sick
When he sticks it out and shoves it up his nose

You can see around his lips
The sticky trail that drips
A pink and fatty slug that grows and grows
But if we're bored in class
He can always make us laugh
When he sticks it out and shoves it up his nose

Our long tongue twisting teacher's
Tongue is like an alien creature
A shell-less slimy snail that shows and glows
He just cannot resist it
The urge to turn and twist it
When he sticks it out and shoves it up his nose

His nostrils open very wide ...
And his tongue comes down the other side

How To Hide At School

I know the secret hidey-holes
The places no one ever goes
Caretakers, cleaners – no one knows
Why I can hide at school

Cupboards and the corridors
Spaces underneath the floors
Places in and out of doors
How I can hide at school

Up above the ceiling tiles
Underneath recycling piles
Behind the teachers' unmarked files
Where I can hide at school

Down inside the staging blocks
Store rooms where I pick the locks
In the lost-property box
When I hide at school

In the curtains in the hall
Just behind the toilet wall
I cannot let you know of all
The ways to hide at school

Practised them since I was five
Places I can hide and skive
It's the way you can survive
If you hide at school

Twelve Inventions To Help You Survive At School

The teacher's lesson lie detector
The secret chocolate bar collector
The answer sheet for SATs reflector

The confiscated toy locator
The extra homework duplicator
The Literacy eradicator

The dinner lady anaesthetiser
The school dinner atomiser
The fact recalling knowledge visor

The X-ray teacher's diary reader
The secret sweets in lesson feeder
The teacher's desk nest maggot breeder

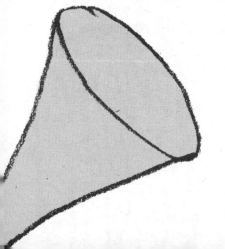

Teacher's Very Quiet Today

Teacher's very quiet today,
hasn't shouted once
but just let us get on with things
in a gentle sort of way.

Several times I caught her gaze
but I wasn't even noticed.
Teacher looks preoccupied
like something's weighing heavy on her mind.

I don't know what it is
but I think I've seen that look before.
The expression seems familiar,
though not in school.

It's more like the look Dad had
when he crashed his new car
or when Mum found out
that Auntie Jo was ill.

Teacher's very quiet today,
hasn't shouted once
but just let us get on with things
in a gentle sort of way.

NIGEL

Nigel sits alone
He isn't too fat
He isn't too thin
He doesn't smell
He doesn't have scruffy clothes
He doesn't talk posh
He isn't a swot
He isn't ugly
And he isn't thick

Nigel's just quiet, shy and average
And Nigel sits alone.

Just Jacko

Jimmy likes Joanne
but Joanne likes Jonathon
who only has eyes for Jane.
Jane likes Joe
but Joe likes Julie.
Julie doesn't know this
and thinks he likes Jenny
so she likes Jeffrey instead.
Jenny likes Jeffrey as well
but Jeffrey likes Judy.
Judy ignores him
As she likes John
but John likes Janet
who in turn likes Jimmy.

Jacko couldn't care less.
He likes football and chocolate best.

Iqbal Doesn't Like School Really

Iqbal doesn't like school really
It's not because he can't do the work
But because some of the other children
Don't seem to like him that much

They call him names and make up jokes about his mum
Everyone laughs – except Iqbal
Everyone laughs – except Iqbal

They all think it's okay because it's only a laugh and a joke
And they don't really mean it anyway
But Iqbal doesn't know that

Iqbal doesn't know that
And because of that
Iqbal doesn't like school really

Fighting Talk

D'youwannafight?
Yeah

Anytime?
Yeah

Anyplace?
Yeah

Anywhere?
Yeah

Four o'clock tonight behind the Co-Op then?
... er

Well?
... ummm

What ?
*I've got to go shopping with my mum tonight
But any other time I'd fight you.*

WASN'T ME

Wasn't me sir, honest sir
Wasn't me, itwozzim.
Wasn't withim sir
Itwozzim sir, honest.
I wasn't withim sir
Wasn't me sir
Wozzim!

I was quite near him though.

PLAYTIME

Hurrah! Yippee! It's playtime, it's playtime!
We're out of the classroom – ace!
No more lessons because it's playtime.
What shall we play? What shall we do?
I don't mind as long as it's fun.
What shall we play at then?
You choose ... no I don't want to choose.
You decide ... I decided last time remember ...
Okay then, let's play that.
You start, no you start, let's play.
Hurrah! Yippee! It's playtime, it's playti ....
Oh no! That was the bell.
It's not playtime any more.

Playtime Footy

It's a game of three halves at our school,
Morning break, lunch and afternoon play.
Down with the sports bag posts,
Thirteen a side and first to thirty wins.

In Summer it's a game of four halves.
You've got to get there early,
Half eight at the very latest
Or else you don't get on the team you want.

Three halves or four,
Some games lasted a week
Monday to Friday
Adding up the scores.

Playground footy, a full match could be
A game of twenty halves,
At least thirteen a side
And first to fifty wins.

Bullies And Their Friends

Bullies have gangs and never walk alone.
They never speak to you one to one,
it's always some little friend who says
"Watch it you're dead! My big mate's going to get
  you right!"

Bullies' friends are always small.
By themselves they're nothing, nobodies
but when they're with their big mates
they think they're big hard tough guy fighters.

Bullies and their friends are always small people inside,
pretending that they're really tough
when really they're frightened nobodies, scared to
  be alone.

If you do catch them alone
they will be just as scared as you might be
and just as likely to walk away silently
as they are to start a fight
because bullies and their friends are cowards.
Bullies and their friends are cowards.

Outsider Inside

I've joined the choir – but I hate singing
I'm a library helper – but I don't like books
I'm in the drama club – but I'm no good on stage

I'm the one who tidies the paints up at break
And asks to do jobs for teacher, any jobs
Because I don't want to go outside

They call me teacher's pet and other names
But I don't mind – not really
Anything's better than going outside

They're Good Friends But ...

Karen is a gossip
Sharon's really mean
Stacey is a sulk
Tracey thinks she's queen

Judy is a fusspot
Trudy is a snob
Penny is a moaner
Jenny is a slob

Annie's mouth almighty
Frannie's far too loud
Polly's really flirty
Holly's far too proud

All of them are good friends
But as you can see
None of them are perfect
So ... meet me!

Bonkers For Conkers

I'm bonkers for conkers
I have a sixty-one-er
Billy's belter battered it
Now it is a gone-er

Fly Away Teacher ...

The plastic flies the sugar cubes disguise
Always give my teacher a surprise
They melt into her tea
Rise up floating instantly
You should see the fear in her eyes!

Thumb-Thing's Up!

If there is one trick that cannot fail
Guaranteed to make your teacher pale
Always lots of shocks and fun
When you show a bloodstained thumb
Complete with bandage and a rusty nail

Mr Radar's Ears

Beep beep beep – everything he hears
Beep beep beep – Mr Radar's ears
Beep beep beep – every whisper, every word
Beep beep beep – every single noise is heard
Beep beep beep – left and right and far and near
Beep beep beep – Mr Radar's ears

The scratchings of the pencils
The creaking of the chairs
The answers that are whispered
The footsteps on the stairs
The crunching of the crisps
The dropping of a pin
The scrunching of the papers
Thrown into the bin
Calculators beeping
The headteacher who's sleeping
Jangling caretaker's keys
All the little things like these

Beep beep beep …

Pencil sharpeners grating
The hinges on the door
The secretary's heels
Clip clopping on the floor

Every nose that's blown or sniffed
Every toilet flushing
The boiler in the basement
That's bubbling and gushing
The sucking of illegal sweets
The shuffling of shoeless feet
Every stifled cough or slurp
Every swallow, every burp

Beep beep beep ...

The nibbling of fingernails
The bouncing of a ball
The distant squeak of plimsolls
Running round the hall
The dinner ladies shouting
The opening of cans
The whoomph of ovens lighting
The rattling of the pans
Every stomach rumbling
Boys' intestines grumbling
Secret wind or ripping breeze
Every little sniff and sneeze

Beep beep beep ...

Lunchpack Flapjack Snack Attack

Lunchtime crunch time canteen chaos
Injuries sustained
Somebody could lose an eye
Someone could get maimed

There's carnage in the canteen
Bruises blue and black
Cereal killer snipers
Flying flapjack snack attack

Three corners, filed and pointed
History in the making
Three angles, sharp, acute
Where martial arts meets baking

Lunch time on the front line
And it's getting out of hand
Get the point and you're out of joint
Triangles should be banned

Risk assessment madness
Why can't they think to warn us
Health and Safety missed the point
That squares have extra corners

A third more dangerous than
The flapjacks snacks triangular
It's so wrong to be oblong
Not right to be rectangular

So ban this flapjack fighting
Before we all descend
Into oatmeal Armageddon
Just where will it end?

Cake A 47's
Ginger ninja bread grenades
Detonating doughnuts
Destruction and decay

Choc chip nun-chuck cookies
Sharpened star shaped shortbread
Sliced fun with those iced buns
Sticking out your forehead

Cornflake crunch catastrophe
Will they stop at nothing?
Rice crispy slice – well, ain't nice
Better watch out for that muffin!

This lethal weapon lunchtime
Dare Health and Safety risk it?
This all out war that's so much more
Than battle with a biscuit

Weapons of molass destruction
Stockpiled on the stack
So dodge the flak
Stay at the back

Just stay off this eaten track
Eye eye – all right jack
Lunch pack flat pack flapjack snack pack
Smack crack flapjack snack attack

The Kitchen Regrets the Inconvenience Caused

Sincere apologies regarding today's menu
We've run out of fat and gristle so steak will have to do.
Last month's cabbage stock ran out yesterday
Sorry for the freshness of the carrots today.

Due to lack of staff everybody's flustered
We haven't had time to add the lumps into the custard.
The gravy isn't sliced, everybody's rushed
You can see which food is which, nothing much is mushed.

The cauliflower is undercooked, this is a warning
We haven't had the time to boil it up all morning.
Because of a power cut we couldn't singe the chips
And the pizza's soft and doesn't shatter into tiny bits.

We're sorry for the quality of food to be consumed
But rest assured tomorrow normal service is resumed.

The Dinner Lady Boot Camp Crew

D-I-N! D-I-N! D-I-DOUBLE-N-E-R!
D-I-N! D-I-N! D-I-DOUBLE-N-E-R!

Dinner lady boot camp crew
We are trained to hassle you
Rough and tough commando troop
We will make your shoulders droop
We don't like you kids at all
Messing up our dining hall

D-I-N! D-I-N! D-I-DOUBLE-N-E-R!
D-I-N! D-I-N! D-I-DOUBLE-N-E-R!

Dinner lady boot camp crews
Bulging muscles and tattoos
Hairy legs and size twelve shoes
You will eat revolting stews
Sausages like doggy doos
Guaranteed to use the loos

D-I-N! D-I-N! D-I-DOUBLE-N-E-R!
D-I-N! D-I-N! D-I-DOUBLE-N-E-R!

We have trained for months and years
We'll have you in floods of tears
We are here to spoil your fun
We are here to get you done
Dinner lady boot camp crew
And we'll get the teachers too

D-I-N! D-I-N! D-I-DOUBLE-N-E-R!
D-I-N! D-I-N! D-I-DOUBLE-N-E-R!

written with David Harmer

The Food of Love

I'm in love with my dinner lady
I see her – my heart skips
I really think she loves me too
She gives me extra chips

Dear Headteacher ...

I'm writing to say sorry about your window that
    was smashed
It wasn't me that did it, but someone from my class

I didn't kick the ball at all, I didn't really know
I didn't see the shot that took it through your
    new window ...

I wasn't even playing, I just happened to be standing
I didn't have a clue where the ball would end up landing

I wasn't really looking, my eyes were closed instead
It wasn't my fault that the ball bounced off my head

If it hadn't hit my head it would just have hit the wall
But you're the one who told me to be standing there
    at all

Everybody laughed at the ricochet deflection,
Well ... everyone but me when the football changed
    direction

Everyone said "Smashing!" and "Look what a beauty!"
But it wasn't my fault, I was just on playground duty.

Deep Dark Secrets in the Staffroom

There are deep dark strange and nasty
secrets in the staffroom
when the teachers escape at break
from the confines of the classroom.
What's behind, what do we find
behind the classroom door?
What lurks inside, what secrets hide
behind the staffroom door?

There are a thousand cups unfinished
all covered in green mould.
Coffee stains and rings remain
where they have overflowed.
Piles of files, unmarked books
and last term's lost reports,
the P.E. teacher's sweaty vest
and lycra cycling shorts.

There are last week's lunch left-overs,
yoghurt pots and crusts,
banana skins and cola tins
all covered in chalk dust.

Examination papers
from nineteen seventy eight
and the Times Ed. Job section
that's ten years out of date.

The bin is overflowing
and it's seeping out the door.
The wind has blown a million sheets
of paper on the floor.
There's paper planes and brown tea stains
from last night's staff meeting.
This place is a downright disgrace
not fit for a pig to eat in.

Inside the fridge half-finished milk
is lumpy and it's glowing.
The cartons are all starting to mutate
and they are growing.
The crockery mountain in the sink
is coated in green lime
and the room that time forgot
is left to rot in gunge and slime.

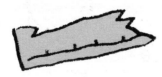

There are deep, dark, strange and nasty
secrets in the staffroom
when the teachers escape at break
from the confines of the classroom.
What's behind, what do we find
behind the staffroom door?
What lurks inside, what secrets hide
behind the staffroom door?

Beware the creatures from this place,
the ones who always say
"No one leaves this classroom
until this mess is cleared away!"
But if you said the same to them
one thing is very clear –
to get the staffroom spick and span
would take at least a year
... or two ... or three ... or four ... or maybe even more!

Shoes

Our headteacher – Mr Hughes
Only has one pair of shoes
Battered, black and boring – he
Has worn them for eternity

Miss has different views on shoes
A thousand boots or heels to choose
Every day we look and learn
Different each day, every term

VISITORS BEWARE

In the corner of the staffroom
Well worn and threadbare
The booby-trapped, elastic-snapped
Collapsing secret chair
Teachers leave it well alone
They know what's lurking there
The buttock-clenching, jacket-wrenching
Never mentioned chair

The only seat that's left at break
So trying to relax
You sink in the ever shrinking
Chair apt to collapse
Your coffee cup shoots ten feet up
Your knees are near your hair
In the folding, overloading
Self-imploding chair

When sitting with the teachers
All visitors beware
The jacket-wrenching, buttock-clenching,
Ever-sinking, ever-shrinking,
Self-imploding, over-loading,
Parping, squeaking, trouser-tweaking
Twisting, turning, non-discerning,
Living, breathing, most deceiving
Booby-trapped, elastic-snapped
Collapsing staffroom chair

The Unseen Queen

Doris cleans the tables
Polishes the floors
Picks up all the rubbish
Closes all the doors
Locks up every window
Turns off every light
Serves and makes refreshments
Every Open Night
Brews the tea for teachers
While the pupils play
Washes all the cups
And puts them all away
Nothing ever happens
When she's not involved
Running things like clockwork
Every problem solved
No one sees her very much
Behind every scene
But Doris rules our school
She's our Unseen Queen.

I Just Don't Trust The Furniture

I just don't trust the furniture
The desks have all got teeth
Grinning fangs inviting
Evilly delighting
At what they could be biting
And dragging down beneath ...

Violet electric light
Bursts in violent blasts
Forked tongue lightning slithers
Like vicious neon rivers
Everybody shivers
Until the storm has passed

No one knows just how or why
But when they start to glow
When open lids are gaping
There is no escaping
The scratching and the scraping
Of the horrors down below

A corridor is opened
A gateway is unfurled
Its gravity commences
To hypnotise the senses
And drag you down defenceless
To its nightmare world

Our Teacher's Great Big Tropical Fish Tank

Our teacher's great big tropical fish tank is huge
Fills up a whole wall in the classroom

He changes the water regularly
It's at exactly the right temperature

There are pebbles, stones, deep-sea wrecks
And sunken treasure chests in the sand

Plants waft gracefully in the gentle currents
And those little bubbles rise to the surface constantly

Yes, our teacher's great big tropical fish tank is huge —
Fills up a whole wall in the classroom

He hasn't got any tropical fish though ...

But the guinea pigs seem quite happy
They like the snorkels, masks and flippers.

Sometimes ... When the Teacher Isn't Looking

Sometimes
When it's quiet and the whole class is working
And the teacher isn't looking ...
We look at the teacher ... not looking.

Sometimes they yawn
Sometimes they rub their eyes
Sometimes they brush dust off their sleeves
Sometimes they stretch Blu-tack and straighten
    paper clips.

Sometimes they doodle
But mostly they go misty-eyed
And stare out of that window daydreaming of summer
No kids, no books, no marking but peace and quiet and
    lazy days.

So when the teacher isn't looking at us
We look at the teacher ... not looking at us.

When The Teacher Turns Their Back

Everyone's a maniac
When the teacher turns their back

Books are toppled stack by stack
Worksheets scattered pack by pack
Lunches opened snack by snack
When the teacher turns their back.

Elastic bands go thwackety thwack
Pens and pencils clickety clack
Rulers twang and flickety flack
When the teacher turns their back.

Someone throws an anorak
Someone flies a plastic mac
Someone's chucking bric-a-brac
When the teacher turns their back.

Patak is whacking Mac and Jack
Matt is smacking Pat and Lak
Everyone's attacking Zack
When the teacher turns their back.

Rubbish scattered from the sack
Paint is splattered from the rack
Red and yellow, green and black
When the teacher turns their back.

Boys and girls have got the knack
A tug of war with stretched Blu-tack
Six feet long and still no slack
When the teacher turns their back.

Victor thinks he's Vlad the Drac
Peter's riding piggyback
Nicola's a natterjack
When the teacher turns their back.

Karl's a kleptomaniac
Thinks it's clever to hijack
Kidnaps Katie's Caramac
When the teacher turns their back.

John looks like a frightened yak
Swinging from the curtain track
To and fro amidst the flak
When the teacher turns their back.

Yakety yakety yakety yak
Quackety quackety quackety quack
Everyone's a maniac
When the teacher – trusting creature –
When the teacher turns their back.

Champion of the School

I'm the loudest burping, armpit honking
Top paper plane making
Best funny face pulling
Double jointed knuckle crackling
Most consistent homework losing
Most inventive earwax moulding
Highest number chip chewing
Biggest bubble gum blowing
Smelliest sweaty sock sniffing
Furthest paper pellet throwing
Most finger nose picking
Long distance bogey flicking
Raspberry blowing, tongue sticking
Ear clipping, bottom kicking
Pimple popping, zit splitting
Wall hitting, slick spitting
Sneezing, wheezing, toe cheesing
Thunderpanted, loud chanted
Champion Of The School !

The Reasons Why

As you already know,
the dog did eat my Art homework
but I can actually tell you the reasons why ...

The sketch of the bone I did was brilliant,
in fact it was so lifelike that Bonzo chewed it
and buried it in the garden

The picture I had painted of the cat
was so realistic that Bonzo attacked it
and ripped it to shreds.

Maybe I shouldn't have used real steak
as part of my sculpture.

The kennel wasn't the best place
to leave my painting to dry.

Dad threw the stick I was carving
for Bonzo to fetch but he didn't want to give it back
and then it snapped when Dad pulled really hard.

So you see, it wasn't entirely my fault
That the dog ate my homework.

There's Nothing Wrong With Crying

It's hard to smile when your dog has died
It's hard to smile when you hurt inside
It's hard to smile when you'd rather hide
There's nothing wrong with crying.

It's hard to laugh when your gran is ill
It's hard to laugh when you feel no thrill
Cos your football team has lost six nil
There's nothing wrong with crying.

It's hard to cheer when your dad is mad
And the tone of his voice makes you feel sad
And you can't recall the fun you've had
There's nothing wrong with crying.

It's hard to cry when things are rough
And the kids around say it's not tough
But I do not believe that stuff
There's nothing wrong with crying.

Dads do it, mums do it
Boys do it, girls do it,
You do it, I do it
You're never the only one to do it
There's nothing wrong with crying
Nothing wrong with crying.

At Christmas ... at Easter

At Christmas
we remember Jesus and Mary and Joseph
and the shepherds and star and the wise men
and the gold and frankincense and myrrh
and how God was born in a stable.

At Easter
we remember eggs.

I Think I'm The Only One

I think I'm the only one
who closes my eyes for the prayers in assembly
but I can't be sure ...
because I think I'm the only one
who closes my eyes for the prayers in assembly.

WHEN MR TOPPING SAYS THE PRAYERS

It's different in assembly
When Mr Topping says the prayers

When some of the other teachers have to lead them
It's just words that they read
Like we do in reading time

They come out in the right order
But you can tell that they're not really interested
And that they don't want to do it

But it's different in assembly
When Mr Topping says the prayers

Just in Case ...

In assembly today we had a visit from the Vicar.
I wasn't really listening,
I was thinking about that goal I scored last night
and then I thought about that girl from Class 6 who's
    really nice
and how Muggo Mills is a bully and smells
when I heard the Vicar say
"... and God sees everything we do, boys and girls ..."

I stopped thinking about goals and girls and grotbags.
Does that mean everything ?
Does he see me pulling faces behind the teachers' backs,
being cheeky to Mum,
blaming things on my little brother,
copying my homework off Jimbo,
giving the dog my teatime cabbage,
picking my nose and wiping it on the chair,
sitting on the loo ...

I hope he didn't see me laughing at that old lady
or the time I put the tortoise on roller skates.
Maybe he blinked when I put salt and pepper in
    Auntie Jean's tea.
Perhaps he wasn't looking when I called the new
    boy that horrible name ...

Just in case he can see everything,
maybe I'll try a bit harder in the future.
Just for a bit anyway.
Just in case.

THE TEACHER'S WINTER WEDNESDAY EVENING

The teacher at home
Leaves the pizza crust at the side of their plate
Dozes in front of soap-opera television
Makes another cup of coffee
In an effort to get
Through the planning and marking
Then watches the midweek film
While praying for a peaceful day tomorrow
And that the Summer holidays could be rearranged
For this week's Friday afternoon

THE FIRST SNOW ON THE PLAYGROUND

Waking up to the scrunching carpet crunch
The photographic negative
The cotton wool icing
The transforming blanket
Where even city centres could be Christmas cards

And every child
Delves into under-stairs cupboards
For winter boots and wellies
Wanting to be the first
The very, very first
To leave their mark
And hear the sound of footprints in the snow
On the playground at school

JOHN'S OK – REALLY?

John's OK really.
It's best when we're on our own though –
Bike riding, telling jokes, doing impressions
    of teachers.
No one mentions his glasses then
Or the way his hair never stays in place,
The fact that sometimes he stutters a bit
Especially if he gets a question wrong.

It's different at school though.
Some of the bigger ones pick on him –
Not really, really nasty –
They don't hit him or anything,
But just keep at him …
On and on and on and on.

I know it makes him upset
But he tries not to cry in front of them.
I know it makes him sad
But I never say much at all.
I just sort of go quiet and keep my head down.

I know I should say something
But if I did …
Well, they might just start on me then.

Mothers' Day Cards

I felt sorry for Samantha
on the day we made Mothers' Day cards.

She doesn't see her mummy much
since she moved away.

She still made a card
but it never got sent.

It was the best one in the class.
Samantha cried at playtime.

It's Hard Being a Jehovah's Witness at Christmas

We don't have Christmas at our house.
Dad says it's because of our religion.
Our church talks about Jesus and we read the Bible
And sing songs all about Jesus.
It does seem strange to me.

So while all the other kids have a concert in assembly
I read in a room by myself.
While they have an end of term party
With cakes and dancing and the Head dressed up as
    Father Christmas
I get to go home early.

I feel a bit left-out really.
Dad says we've got to be strong about what we believe.
It's not easy being strong sometimes.

THE DAY THAT MISS WENT MISSING
AND SIR JUST WASN'T THERE

Classroom Six completely changed
The furniture was rearranged
The atmosphere was different, something new was in the air
Playtime started way too soon
And lasted till the afternoon
The day that Miss went missing and Sir just wasn't there.

Where the blackboard should have been
There's a giant TV screen
Dayglo cartoons hypnotise with fluorescent glare
Lessons all were history
No English, Maths or Geography
The day when Miss went missing and Sir just wasn't there.

All computers have been set
For surfing on the internet
Fingers click on keyboards and printers start to whirr
There's burger bars and take-aways
Where there once were art displays
The day that Miss went missing and Sir just wasn't there.

A thudding, scudding bassline pounds
Speakers quake and shake the grounds
Strobe lights strike like lightning as the rhythm starts to blare
Posters and graffiti art
Replace the Maths and spelling chart
The day that Miss went missing and Sir just wasn't there.

Look your best and feel real cool
With sunbeds and jacuzzi pool
Complete with beauty salon for manicures and hair
Hoops for playing basketball
Hang tall on every classroom wall
The day that Miss went missing and Sir just wasn't there.

Instead of desks there's fruit machines
Instead of text books – magazines
Instead of hard-backed benches a soft and comfy chair
The only homework seems to be
Soaps and gameshows on TV
The day that Miss went missing and Sir just wasn't there.

The old regime was obsolete
When our arrangements were complete
The old was out, the new was in, so teachers just beware!
Pupil power rules this school
To make it fun and make it cool
The day that Miss went missing and Sir just wasn't there.

I WOULD WIN THE GOLD IF THESE WERE OLYMPIC SPORTS

Bubble-gum blowing
X-Box watching
Late morning snoring
Homework botching

Bed quilt ruffling
Little brother teasing
Pizza demolishing
Big toe cheesing

Insult hurling
Tantrum throwing
Infinite blue
Belly button fluff growing

Late night endurance
Laptop gazing
Non attentive open jawed
Eyeball glazing

Ultimate volume
Decibel blaring
Long distance marathon
Same sock wearing

Recognise these sports
Then meet ...
Me – The Champ
Apathetic athlete!

DON'T GO IN THE CHANGING ROOMS

Rancid socks and deep heat fumes
Fumigate the changing rooms!

Shattered shin pads, stained with blood
Battered boots and last year's mud

Voodoo dolls of referees
Sucked and spat-out orangees

Broken toe nails, bits of plaster
Squashed bananas, squished up pasta

Crumbled biscuits on the floor
Rude graffiti on the door

Shower gel that's spilt and set
Slippy soap, squashed and wet

Goalie glove – by itself
Sprays and ointments on the shelf

Bandages and toilet rolls
Towels fester, growing mould

The full-back's underpants that stink
Striker's hair bands – bright and pink

Rancid socks and deep heat fumes
DON'T GO IN THE CHANGING ROOMS!

Getting The Preparation Right

10 king size bars of chocolate
9 packets of crisps
8 jam doughnuts
7 sweet and sour gobstoppers
6 packs of Megdubblebubble Bubble Gum
5 cans of pop – fizzy
4 tubes of mints
3 choc chip muffins
2 apples
1 cheese and tomato sandwich

Yes.
Should be enough for the school trip.
This afternoon.

We Want To Go Where We Want To Go

We don't want trips to the country
We don't want to stroll up hills
We don't want to study flowers
We don't want to hike round fields

We want to go where we want to go
On a school trip that is ace
Fly up in a sonic rocket
For a week in outer space

We want to go to Disneyland
With all the shows and rides
Thrills and spills of tracks and wheels
Churning our insides

We want to go to festivals
Dance to the rock-and-roll beats
Or a free trip to the cinema
With popcorn, drinks and sweets

We want a school trip to the moon
Where no one else can reach us
But most of all we want to go
And leave behind the teachers!

It's Raining on the Trip

It's raining on the trip
Raining on the trip
Drip drip drip
It's raining on the trip.

It's never going to stop
Never going to stop
Drop drop drop
It's never going to stop.

I haven't got a coat
Haven't got a coat
Splish splash splosh
I'm going to get soaked.

Under Ruth's waterproof
Under Pat's pacamac
Under Ella's umbrella
Under Mac's anorak
Things aren't getting much better
Things are getting much wetter

I think it's going to flood
Think it's going to flood
Thud thud thud
I think it's going to flood

The clouds are getting dark
Clouds are getting dark
If it rains much more
Then we're going to need an ark.

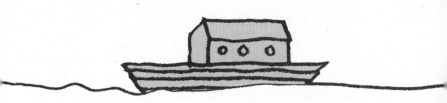

The Carrier Bag That No One Claims

It's driving everyone insane
Steaming up the windowpanes
There's a fuss on the bus – all complain
The carrier bag that no one claims

It lives and breathes with several strains
Of germs and other unknown stains
And life that science can't explain
The carrier bag that no one claims

Eyes and nostrils wince in pain
It reeks of sweaty clogged-up drains
And smells like stuff you flush with chains
The carrier bag that no one claims

SHORT VISIT - LONG STAY

Our school trip was a special occasion
But we never reached our destination
Instead of the zoo
I was locked in the loo
In an M62 service station

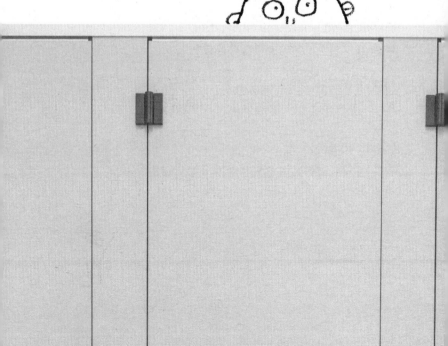

I Don't Want to go to Big School

I don't want to go to big school
I don't want to leave.

I like it here, my class is great
And my teacher's lovely.

I don't want to go to big school
I don't want to be small again.

Teachers at big school shout
And I'm scared of getting lost.

I'm worried about my timetable
And remembering everything.

I don't like the playground
And I haven't got my desk, my special place.

I want to grow up
But I don't want to leave and go to big school
Just yet.

First Day of the Summer Holidays

Time to put the pens to bed
Time to put the books away
Time to hide the uniform
We're on Summer Holiday!

Time to switch my alarm clock off
Time to sleep and overlay
Time to lock the homework up
We're on Summer Holiday!

Time to zip my schoolbag up
And in the cupboard let it stay
With my boring shoes for school
We're on Summer Holiday!

Time for trainers, time for jeans
Time for riding on my bike
Time for football all day long
Time for doing what I like.

Time for camping out in tents
Time for having lots of fun
Time for swimming, time for grinning,
Eating ice-creams in the sun.

Time for playing hide and seek
Time for climbing high up trees
Time to rope swing over ditches
Time for scratched and dirty knees.

Time for going out with mates
Time for playing any game
Time for watching DVDs
All day long if it should rain.

Time for tennis, time for cricket,
Time for friends to come and call
Time for doing everything
Or doing nothing much at all.

Time for laughter, time for jokes,
Time for fun and time to play
Time to fool so goodbye school!
We're on Summer Holiday!

Paul Cookson has worked as a poet for over 25 years, visited over 4,000 schools, written and edited over 45 collections of poetry and sold over a million books. He is still not very good at Maths.

His work has appeared on national radio and TV, at festivals, and in libraries, and he travels internationally to perform his work and lead workshops.

A great collaborator – he is man of several double acts. With David Harmer, he is half of Spill The Beans. With Stan Cullimore, he plays ukulele and even sings. With Stewart Henderson – he does all the above. You Tube can verify it all!

He is the Poet-in-Residence for the National Football Museum.

When not touring, performing, leading workshops for children and teachers, Paul lives in Retford with his wife, two children, a dog and a growing family of ukuleles.

For more details visit www.paulcooksonpoet.co.uk or follow him on twitter – paulcooksonpoet

MORE POETRY BY PAUL COOKSON
PUBLISHED BY FRANCES LINCOLN CHILDREN'S BOOKS

Meet sensational scorers, dependable defenders, great
goalkeepers and fanatical fans like Great Gran. Find out
who always shouts at the ref, what is scary about being in
the wall, where the wasp flew and why you shouldn't put
mums in goals. Every aspect of the football season and
more are brilliantly brought to life by poet and
football fan Paul Cookson.

'A sure-fire hit. ... A superb, easily accessible and very
attractive book.' – *School Librarian*

Frances Lincoln titles are available from all good bookshops.
You can also buy books and find out more about your favourite titles,
authors and illustrators on our website: www.franceslincoln.com